Founder's Pocket Guide: Convertible Debt

1x1MEDIA

Simple, quick answers, all in one place.

By

Stephen R. Poland

1x1 Media
Asheville, North Carolina
United States

Care has been taken to verify the accuracy of information in this book. However, the authors and publisher cannot accept responsibility for consequences from application of the information in this book, and makes no warranty, expressed or implied, with respect to its content.

Trademarks: Some of the product names and company names included in this book have been used for identification purposes only and may be trademarks or registered trade names of their respective manufacturers and sellers. The author and publisher disclaim any affiliation, association, or connection with, or sponsorship or endorsement by, such owners.

ISBN 978-1-938162-05-3

© 2017 by 1x1 Media, LLC

email: info@1x1media.com

website : www.1x1media.com

Table of Contents

Founder's Pocket Guide: Convertible Debt

"Is it scarier to launch your startup now, or wake up in 5 years feeling the regret of not at least trying?"

– Mitchell Harper, co-founder of Bigcommerce

What the Founder's Pocket Guide Series Delivers

We developed the *Founder's Pocket Guide* series to provide quick answers to common questions encountered by entrepreneurs. Consider the following dilemmas:

> "I sort of know **what startup equity is**, but really don't understand the details, and I have an investor interested in my company. Where do I start?"

> "My co-founder said we need to **build a cap table to track our equity ownership**—how do we get started?"

> "My co-founders and I need to determine **how to divide the ownership** of our startup, but how can we be certain we get it right?"

> "I've heard that **convertible debt is a good funding structure for early-stage startups**. What is convertible debt and how do I approach potential investors with a funding pitch?"

The *Founder's Pocket Guide* series addresses each of the topics in a concise and easy to reference format.

Look for these current titles at www.1x1media.com:

- *Founder's Pocket Guide: Founder Equity Splits*

- *Founder's Pocket Guide: Cap Tables*

- *Founder's Pocket Guide: Startup Valuation*

- *Founder's Pocket Guide: Terms Sheets and Preferred Shares*

- *Founder's Pocket Guide: Raising Angel Capital*

Disclaimers

The content in this guide is not intended as legal, financial, or tax advice and cannot be relied upon for any purpose without the services of a qualified professional. With that disclaimer in mind, here's our position on how to best use the guidance provided in this work.

Great entrepreneurs use all the resources available to them, making the best decisions they can to mitigate risk and yet move ahead with the most important tasks in their roadmaps. This process includes consulting lawyers, CPAs, and other professionals with deep domain knowledge when necessary.

Great entrepreneurs also balance a strong do-it-yourself drive with the understanding that the whole team creates great innovations and succeeds in bringing great products to the world. Along those lines, here's a simple plan for the scrappy early-stage founder who can't afford to hire a startup lawyer or CPA to handle all of the tasks needed to close a funding deal or form the startup:

> **1. Educate yourself on what's needed.** Learn about startup equity structures and issues, legal agreements, financing structures, and other company formation best practices, and then;

> **2. Get your lawyer involved**. Once you thoroughly understand the moving parts and have completed some of the work to the best of your ability, pay your startup-experienced lawyer or other professional to advise you and finalize the legal contracts.

With this self-educating and money-saving sequence in mind, let's dig in to this *Founder's Pocket Guide.*

Introducing This Pocket Guide

The goal of this guide is to help you understand the key moving parts of the convertible debt funding structure. The book also serves as an easy reference for the most common terms and calculations related to convertible debt.

Critical Early Funding. The convertible debt funding structure has become popular among angel groups and well-known startup accelerators such as Y Combinator and Tech Stars. Convertible debt provides a quick way to inject much needed cash into an early stage venture. At the same time, a convertible debt structure offers the investors a mechanism to share in the success of the startup from a very early stage, maximizing the potential return on investment.

Bridging a Gap. Convertible debt also benefits startup founders seeking to bridge the gap between funding rounds. As you will learn in this guide, convertible debt offers an option to delay establishing a pre-money valuation—a step you would prefer to get around if you're anticipating a timeframe of a few months until the next equity round. (You want to avoid too many valuations within a brief time period.)

Expanding on these fundraising concepts, this *Founder's Pocket Guide* helps startup founders learn:

- **What convertible debt is** and how it can be an important fundraising structure.

- **Key terms and definitions** associated with convertible debt, such as conversion triggers, valuation caps, and conversion discounts.

- **Key advantages and disadvantages** of using convertible debt as a funding structure.

- **How investors view the convertible debt**, and what their expectations are for early-stage investment deals.

- **Simple math** for calculating the impact of conversion discount rates and resulting equity ownership on conversion.

- **Example convertible debt deals** illustrating how convertible debt benefits both founders and investors alike.

Pro Tips

To further help guide you through the in's and outs of convertible debt funding, you'll find useful tips throughout this guide that provide deeper insights, insider tips, and additional explanations.

1

Convertible Debt Fundamentals

In this section we'll review the fundamentals of convertible debt, including terminology, basic calculations, advantages and disadvantages. Digging deeper, we'll cover how to use convertible debt funding to delay establishing a valuation, and how to make a good estimate of how much to raise in a convertible debt round.

What Is Convertible Debt?

In a convertible debt investment deal (also referred to as a convertible note), the investor makes a loan to the company (the debt), and that loan converts into equity at some point in the future, with an extra bonus to the investor for taking on higher risk of the early-stage startup.

When founders issue a convertible note, all parties typically assume that the startup will be raising additional funding rounds from experienced angel or VC investors. The graphic on the next page illustrates an example convertible note funding timeline for a startup.

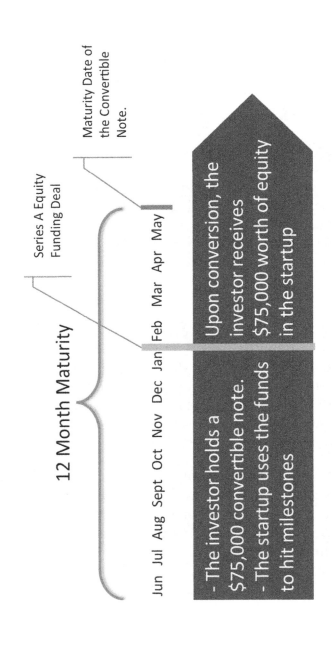

An example convertible debt funding timeline.

When you negotiate an equity deal with later stage investors, a valuation will be negotiated and placed on the company, establishing a share price for the new investors' shares. The share price and valuation provide the inputs needed to perform the convertible note conversion, calculating how many shares the note holder receives for his/her original "loan" to the startup. A detailed example of a note conversation appears at the end of this guide.

To better understand how convertible debt works, consider the following basic components of a convertible debt deal:

- **Delayed Valuation.** Convertible debt provides a method to raise money without putting a valuation on the company at the time when you issue the debt. For an early stage startup that needs more time to bring its product to market, setting a realistic valuation can be tough. So the longer you can delay setting a valuation, the more leverage you will have to raise money later.

- **Interest Rate Earned.** The holder of the convertible note, earns interest on the note, just like a bank that charges loan interest. The startup does not actually make payments on the loan or pay interest. The interest accrues over the term of the note and gets added into the total value of the note when it converts to the new class of shares negotiated in the next investment round.

- **Conversion Trigger.** Typically, the convertible notes converts at a defined "trigger event," most often when the startup raises its first valued round, meaning you and the next round of investors agree on a pre-money valuation for the startup. The note then converts into X number of preferred shares, with the same rights as established in the negotiations with the new investors for the valued round.

- **Discount Rate Sweetener.** Convertible notes also carry a discount rate that sweetens the deal for the note holder. The note holder gets to buy the newly valued stock at a discount from the stock price associated with the valuation established with the new investors, thus getting more shares for the money. Discounts typically range from 15% to 25%.

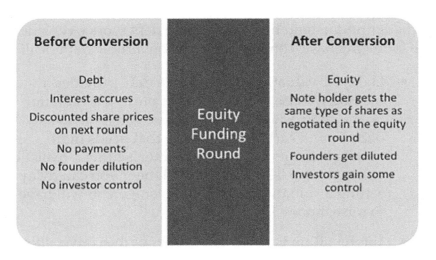

Before Conversion	Equity Funding Round	After Conversion
Debt		Equity
Interest accrues		Note holder gets the same type of shares as negotiated in the equity round
Discounted share prices on next round		
No payments		Founders get diluted
No founder dilution		Investors gain some control
No investor control		

Funding Your Startup with Convertible Debt

Startup founders use several funding structures to secure the capital they need to get their ventures off the ground. They move from personal sources such as savings and credit cards to larger sources of funds such as friends and family loans, and ultimately to equity investments from angels and venture capital firms (VCs). The graphic on the next page illustrates the typical funding progression:

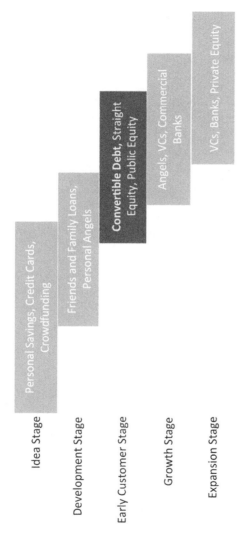

Idea Stage — Personal Savings, Credit Cards, Crowdfunding

Development Stage — Friends and Family Loans, Personal Angels

Early Customer Stage — **Convertible Debt**, Straight Equity, Public Equity

Growth Stage — Angels, VCs, Commercial Banks

Expansion Stage — VCs, Banks, Private Equity

Typical startup funding stages and funding sources.

Drilling Down to Convertible Debt. The table on the next page shows how the convertible debt option fits in with other funding options. Notice that founders typically use a combination of personal funds and friends and family funds to get their new ventures started, and then move to more sophisticated sources of capital such as angel investors.

Startup Stage	Investors	Investment Type	Investment Amount	Valuation
1. Idea	Founders Round	Personal Funds	$50,000	Not needed
2. Development	Friends and Family Round	Simple Loan	$30,000	Not needed
3. Early Customers	1st Angel Round	Convertible Note	$150,000	Not needed
4. Growth	2nd Angel Round	Equity	$250,000	$1,500,000
5. Scaling	VC Round 1 (Series A)	Equity	$1,500,000	$4,000,000
6. Exit Ready	VC Round 2 (Series B)	Equity	$3,000,000	$9,500,000

Convertible debt is often used in early-stage angel funding deals.

Founder's First Encounter with Convertible Debt. The term convertible debt is not a common term used among casual startup supporters such as friends and family members, but it is a common theme in the organized startup investing world. Many independent angel investors and organized angel investment groups are willing to use the convertible debt structure to inject funds into early-stage startups.

The startups may be too early in their evolution to establish a reasonable pre-money valuation, but investors are intrigued enough and want to get involved very early in the startup's existence—convertible debt structure makes it possible for investors to get involved immediately, and ultimately participate in the success of the startup later. See the later section called "Advantages of Funding with Convertible Debt" for more details why investors often favor this funding structure.

Startup Funding Terminology

To keep these convertible debt funding components in perspective, let's review several additional key terms associated with startup funding and convertible debt structure:

- **Equity.** The ownership of the startup—who owns how much. In the most common sequence, the founders own 100% equity of the startup at formation, then give up chunks of ownership to outside investors in exchange for cash investments. Portions of equity are also given to key employees in the form of stock options as additional compensation for their contributions to the startup's efforts. If the startup gets acquired by a larger company (called an exit), the equity ownership percentage determines how much each person or investment entity gets paid.

- **Pre-money Valuation.** The value placed on a startup before an investment round. The pre-money valuation is a key point of negotiation between founders and equity investors.

- **Post-money Valuation.** The value of the startup after the investment round. The investment amount + the pre-money valuation = the post-money valuation.

- **Raise or Round (Investment Round).** The process and result of raising money for your startup is called a *round* or a *raise*. Depending on whether you are at the beginning stages of the money raising process, or have just put an investor's money in the bank, each round goes by a particular name or designation, such as seed round or Series A round.

- **Founder Dilution.** The amount of ownership given up by startup founders, expressed as a percentage— "the founders are willing to accept a 20% dilution in exchange for a $200,000 angel fund investment."

- **Investor Dilution.** Founders are not the only stakeholders that give up equity as new investors come into the funding picture. Existing investors can also be required to withstand a reduction in their ownership percentage in the startup. If the startup raises multiple rounds of equity investment, early investors will give up some ownership to new investors. Anti-dilution rights attached to preferred shares are one way investors attempt to limit their exposure to dilution.

- **Priced Round.** Occurs when the startup closes an equity investment deal ro round with investors. During the process, the valuation of the company is established and the price per share of company stock is calculated. Prior to a startup's first equity fundraising deal, the price per share of stock is set very low (typically $0.0001 per share), or otherwise unpriced. In the convertible debt context, the next priced round is often the key event that triggers the note to convert to equity.

- **Down Round.** When founders accept an equity investment at a valuation lower than the previously established valuation. Such a round establishes that the company is worth less now than it was at the previous investment round. See the later section called "Understanding Down Rounds" for more details.

- **Seed Round.** In common usage, a seed round can be any early investment in a startup used to start the company and create its first products or services. Investments by the founders themselves, friends and family, or other supporters associated with the entrepreneurs who are starting the company can all qualify as seed rounds. In contrast, the high tech Silicon Valley definition of seed round is a bit different. Many large venture capital firms (VCs) have established seed funds with the purpose of backing very early innovations (almost to the point of experiments) that can disrupt very large industries. The amounts invested in seed rounds by these VC seed funds are sometimes large ($1, $2, or even $3 million), as compared to angel funding rounds in the sub $1 million range.

- **Series A, Series B, etc.** Series A is a term used to mean many things, but typically, a Series A is the first VC-level investment round. Additional investments from institutional investors follow the same pattern: Series B, Series C, and so on. Also note that VCs are in the business of investing other institutions money, not personal money from angels or friends and family investors.

- **VC.** Short for venture capital, VCs are large investment funds seeking out high growth startups that have proven new technology and new markets. Venture capitalists are investing other people's money, from sources such as private foundations, pension plans, university capital funds, and so on.

 **Understanding the Impact of Convertible Debt on Future Funding Rounds**

Be sure to include the convertible note loan amount in your cap table calculations. The note amount doesn't immediately influence your founder's equity position, but you don't want to leave it out of the list of funding sources and amounts. When you start lining up later-stage equity funding, investors will want to know what your existing funding picture looks like. For more detail on startup capitalization tables, look for the *Founder's Pocket Guide: Startup Cap Tables* at www.1x1media.com.

What Convertible Debt Implies

When considering raising startup capital in the form of convertible debt, be sure to keep the big picture in mind. An investor makes the convertible debt loan to your startup with the expectation that the loan will convert to equity at your next funding round. This structure means several things:

- **There Will Be a Next Funding Round.** The investor believes that you will be successful raising equity capital in a future funding round.

- **Near-term Timing.** The timeframe expectation for the next funding round is typically 12 to 24 months. Investors expect that the funds provided by the convertible debt will carry the startup through to the next funding round.

- **Exit Potential.** The convertible debt investor believes that your startup has the potential to get acquired (an exit) by a larger company sometime in the future. Exits are the primary mechanism for rewarding investors and generating a healthy return on their investments.

- **High Growth Potential.** Convertible debt funding is best suited to high growth startups that intend to exit. Lifestyle or bootstrap startup founders who wish to maintain ownership over a long period of time should seek funding structures that are not dependent on equity deals and the future sale of the startup. Crowdfunding, friends and family loans, or profit sharing agreements are better options for the bootstrap entrepreneur.

This graphic illustrates an example of how these major events may play out over the life of the startup:

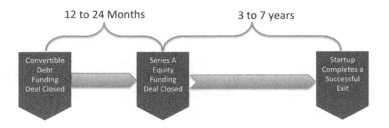

When To Use Convertible Debt

There are two times in your startup's lifecycle when a convertible debt funding structure is best suited:

Early in the Life of the Startup. Convertible debt funding can fuel early stage milestones such as building early version of your product, forming your core startup team, and engaging with early customers. All of these milestones serve to validate your assumptions about your product and customers.

The delayed valuation feature of a convertible debt deal favors many early-stage startups. There are a great many unknowns that make establishing a valuation difficult— what are the ideal market niches for your product, how does your business and revenue model work, what is the status of IP such as patent and key domain names, and so on. Even with many unknowns, some investors will like the potential of your company and want to get in early by investing via a convertible note.

As your startup matures, many of the unknowns become clear, making it possible to secure the next round of equity funding, thus triggering the convertible debt to convert to equity.

As a Bridge to the Next Funding Round. Many times a startup will need a small amount of money to keep the startup going until the next round of funding is completed. The timing of events in the life of startup is never perfect. Equity funding rounds don't close when you expect, key milestones take longer to hit, signing that marquee customer drifted on by an extra two months. A convertible note bridge loan is one option to help fill the time/money gaps that occur.

For example, a startup raises $150,000 in convertible debt to cover the next three months while the next equity round of $3 million is finalized. The $150,000 convertible note holders will piggyback on the next round deal, typically receiving the same type of stock shares and other deal terms (valuation, preferred share rights, etc.) negotiated in the $3 million equity round.

Advantages of Funding with Convertible Debt

The convertible debt funding structure provides entrepreneurs a number of advantages over more complex equity funding structures, including:

Speed. Because a company valuation and other deal points do not need to be established or negotiated, convertible notes provide a faster way for founders to raise money. In an equity funding deal (also called a "priced round," many details are negotiated—including valuation, equity percentages, preferred share rights, and more. These all take time to work out. A convertible debt deal, on the other hand requires agreement on only a few deal points, enabling the parties to close the deal quickly.

Delayed Valuation. As mentioned earlier, convertible debt funding provides a method to raise money without putting a valuation on the company at the time when you issue the debt. The primary reason you establish a valuation for your startup is that you are selling shares to equity investors, usually angel investors or VCs that invest in startups.

Lower Legal Fees. As compared to closing an equity funding deal, a convertible debt agreement typically requires fewer legal documents to execute, therefore limiting the billable hours your startup's lawyer incurs.

Using your startup lawyer to review simple fill-in-the-blanks convertible debt funding paperwork can be relatively low cost—in the $1,000 to $2,000 range at most. In contrast, legal work for a complete Series A equity funding round can run $20,000 to $50,000, or more.

The Right Time for Housekeeping

There are several startup housekeeping steps that founders tend to put off until they are forced by advisors or investors to tackle them. Tasks such as detailing the startup's corporate bylaws, putting founders' equity agreements in writing, assigning IP ownership to the startup, all make the list of items we tend to delay if possible. Taking on outside investors forces completion of these tasks. When you begin to take other people's money, whether in the form of convertible debt, equity, or even simple loans, make the time to get your corporate house in order. Everybody will benefit, and you can eliminate any snags that could kill a later funding deal.

A Rolling Raise. Full-blown equity funding deals require many details to be worked out between founders and investors. Negotiations cause delays and lawyers get involved. Founders burn a lot of time, sometimes many months, before any money shows up in the bank. In contrast, convertible debt funding offers a structure where funding can be raised a chunk at a time, often called a rolling raise. The startup can close smaller portions of a convertible debt raise over several months, as each investor is ready to ante up.

Find an investor ready to commit to a portion of your convertible debt raise, sign the paperwork, and put the money to work. From there, continue to find additional convertible debt investors to complete your funding round.

With the rolling raise structure, you may choose to set a threshold of convertible debt funding to close before spending any of the newly raised funding. For example, if you are raising a total of $500,000 in the form of convertible debt, you might select $250,000 as an appropriate threshold to raise before consuming any committed funds. Such thresholds give investors some comfort that you can reach a level of fundraising success before spending their money. Once you've raised your threshold amount, use the cash to begin hitting milestones, and continue to raise the remaining convertible debt round, another $250,000 in this example.

The following graphic shows how this example might play out. Also note that even though several investors are involved in the convertible debt raise, the total effort of raising $500,000 is considered one funding round.

Investor Name	Committed Amounts	Total Raised So Far
Investor 1	$100,000	$100,000
Investor 2	$75,000	$175,000
Investor 3	$25,000	$200,000
Investor 4	$50,000	$250,000
Investor 5	$75,000	$325,000
Investor 5	tbd	-
Investor 6	tbd	-
Total Convertible Debt Target		$500,000

Founders set a threshold of $250k before funds raised can be tapped.

Founders can use convertible debt to raise money in stages.

Disadvantages of Funding with Convertible Debt

There are a few disadvantages to using convertible debt as a funding structure. The following sections review the convertible debt downsides to keep in mind as you build your funding plan:

Unpriced Rounds for Investors. From the investor perspective, a convertible debt round can be undesirable. Because there is no valuation (and therefore no share price) and no initial exchange of shares for the investment, the investor does not know how much equity s/he will get for the cash invested. Remember, a convertible note is primarily a loan to the startup until it converts to equity at some later point in time. In a priced round where a pre-money valuation is agreed on, the investor knows exactly how much equity is being purchased. The opportunity for an investor to get invested in a hot startup very early, potentially realizing large returns if the startup is successful offsets this disadvantage.

Debt Instrument. A convertible debt investment carries the legal implications of debt. Under most state laws debt holders (lenders) are first in line to get paid back in the case of business liquidation. Whether it's the intent of the founders and investors, the loan to the business establishes an obligation of a cash payback including the principal and interest established in the convertible note. If the startup is unable to raise an equity round, the convertible debt obligation must be dealt with somehow—the section "Dealing with Convertible Debt Timing Issues" reviews the options.

Collateral. Like conventional loans, a convertible debt loan can include clauses that list the assets of the business as collateral for the loan. Again, the true intent of the convertible note deal is not to establish a loan that is paid back or secured by collateral in the event of default. The intent is to help the founders build early success and raise additional capital in the form of equity investment. If your investor requests a collateral clause, be sure to limit the wording to include the assets of the startup only, and not include personal assets of the founders.

Note Holder Approval. More complex convertible debt legal documents include clauses that require the founders to get the approval of the note holders (the investors) prior to the startup to taking on additional debt, or even sometimes other forms of financing. You don't want to have to go back to debt holders to get signatures in order to raise more funds for your new venture. Avoid such strong approval rights if possible.

Conversion Triggers Don't Happen. One of the most common downsides of convertible note financing is reaching the maturity date of the convertible note before an equity deal is completed. If the startup is unable to close an equity deal and the convertible debt maturity date is near, you must renegotiate and extend the term of the convertible note with the note holders. This can be as simple as agreeing to move the maturity date out by X months. However, more sensitive investors might bristle at the issue and drill into why you have not closed an equity round yet.

See the section called "Dealing with Convertible Debt Timing Issues" for more options for dealing with approaching maturity dates.

Why Delaying Valuation is a Good Idea

There are a number of reasons why delaying equity funding, and consequently a valuation, is advisable:

Issuing Stock to Investors is Expensive. Establishing a valuation and completing the legal and business steps needed to issue stock shares to investors is time consuming and expensive. Even simplified sets of legal documents and the associated lawyer input and review can cost a startup $10,000 to 15,000. Using other early stage funding structures such as convertible debt, crowdfunding, and simple friends and family loans can help a new venture achieve early milestones and increase its valuation before taking on outside equity investors.

Off the Shelf Equity Funding Documents

Some startup support organizations like the Y Combinator accelerator program (www.ycombinator.com) and 500 Startups in Austin Texas (www.500startups.com) offer free sets of simplified legal documents that can cut the cost of issuing stock to investors. Whether you are delaying the equity question by using a convertible debt or jumping straight to an equity for cash scenario, be sure to check out these cheaper, faster, alternatives to starting from zero with your startup attorney.

Founder Dilution. Raising equity funding and setting a valuation too early in the startup's lifecycle can cause the founders to give up too much ownership in the new venture. Early-stage startups often have very few validations or accomplishments to help justify a reasonable valuation that preserves founder ownership levels.

The following thought equation and graphic helps visualize the pitfall of establishing a valuation too early:

Few validations = Low valuation
= Founders get heavy dilution

The graphic on the next page shows how the valuation and raise amount influence founder equity.

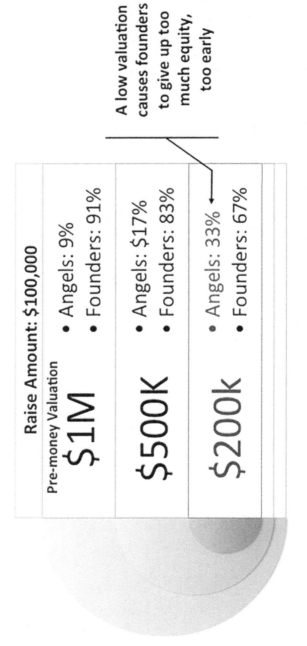

Raise Amount: $100,000

Pre-money Valuation

$1M
- Angels: 9%
- Founders: 91%

$500K
- Angels: $17%
- Founders: 83%

$200k
- Angels: 33%
- Founders: 67%

A low valuation causes founders to give up too much equity, too early

Raising $100,000 on a low valuation causes founders to give up too much.

Taxes. Establishing a valuation sets the price per share for the company stock. At formation of the startup an arbitrarily low starting share price is established, say $0.0001 per share. When a valuation is negotiated with outside investors, the share price increases, say to $0.10 per share. As a result, the founder's (and other stakeholders) paper value of ownership just increased by 1,000 times—the IRS likes to tax such gains. The list of rules for how founder stock is taxed is too long to cover here, but founders should consider filing an 83(b) Election with the IRS. By filing this form, founders are electing to be taxed at the time the purchase their founder's stock (the $0.0001 share price in our example), and therefore avoiding paying for the share price increase until you actually sell you shares.

Options Pricing and Housekeeping. Stock option incentive plans are often created at the same time as the first equity round (when the valuation is established and investor injects cash into the company). Once stock options are granted to employees and other stakeholders, the IRS requires the startup to perform additional housekeeping, such as a 409A valuation. Delaying valuation and the setup of an options incentive plan defers some corporate housekeeping to a time when the founders have more bandwidth and funds to support such tasks.

Investor Control Issues. Bringing in outside investors often means startup founders agree to give up some level of control. Investors typically require preferred shares that give the investor(s) certain rights, such as having a say in future fundraising, executive compensation, and the composition of the board of directors. While these bits of control are often beneficial to inexperienced founders, keeping the complexity to a minimum is usually the best plan until the startup is ready to grow by taking on outside investors and the associated inputs.

How Much to Raise Using Convertible Notes

Deciding how much to raise using convertible debt is best accomplished by building a detailed funding plan. The following steps outline the general process:

1. *Build a Roadmap.* Determine the rough phases of your startup roadmap. Include major milestones that when achieved increase the valuation of the company.

2. *Estimate the Development Budget.* Make educated guesses about the budget/funding needed to complete the subtasks in each milestone of the roadmap.

3. *Calculate the Burn Rate.* Make estimates about the ongoing monthly expenses needed to keep the startup alive during the phases outlined in your roadmap.

4. *Set a Target Equity Funding Date.* Based on the major milestone spending and cash burn funding required, establish the total amount of convertible debt that will enable you to reach key milestones AND convince equity investors to commit the next round of funding required to grow the venture. The convertible debt raise amount will need to carry you to the target equity funding date.

Once you've made good guesses about the investment needed to reach significant milestones, create a detailed use of funds document that details your assumptions for investors.

A well thought out use of funds plan should include:

- How much have you invested so far?

- How much will you need for this round?

- When you will need it?

- What you are going to use the money for, that is, which milestones will the investment enable you to hit?

- When will you need additional investment, or can you reach a self-sustaining level of cash flow?

In the case of an idea-stage startup, the primary use of early funding is to reach significant milestones that are impressive enough to convince the next round equity investors, or secure enough paying customers to reach positive cash flow and self-fund ongoing growth.

The chart on the next page shows a simplified version of a funding roadmap, and the following startup scenario illustrates what each funding round might look like:

Jan - Mar	Apr - Jun	Jul - Dec	Jan - Jun	Jul -->
Startup Formation	App Coding	Local Launch	Add New Colleges	National Launch
Founders Round	F&F Round	Angel Round	Super Angel Round	VC Series A Round
$7,500	$25,000	$150,000	$600,000	$3,000,000

Funding Scenario. Two college buddies, Mark and Jack, have started the coding of a mobile social gaming app. The game uses location aware features, specific landmarks, and other local information on college campuses to create an ongoing campus-wide scavenger hunt environment. The app is so popular on the campus that the startup founders are getting offers from local bars and pizza joints to advertise or sponsor the app. The founders don't have a clear revenue model for the free app yet, but they are adding a great many users, so they know they're onto something big.

Founders Round- $7,500 from Personal Savings. As the co-founders begin to ramp up their app, designing its basic functionality and game play, they start the early steps needed to formalize their startup entity. An initial contribution of cash from each co-founder provides early funding to pay an experienced startup lawyer to guide them through the incorporation process and complete the essential steps of startup formation, such as assigning IP to the startup and creating founders vesting agreements.

Friends and Family (F&F) Round - $25,000 Simple Loans. A deal is structured as a simple loan with the uncle of one of the founders. These funds help the founders continue to develop the app and begin exploring how to integrate the advertising revenue model into the business.

Angel Round - $150,000 Convertible Debt: Six months later the first angel round closes in the form of a convertible note. The note will convert to equity on the next funding round, and the angels will receive the same class of shares as the next super angel round.

Super Angel Round - $600,000. After another six months, the startup continues adding new customers at two additional college campuses. The first angel group helps bring in two additional angel funds to build a total round of $600,000 equity investment in the startup. The previous $150,000 angel investment converts to equity in this funding round.

VC Series A Round - $3 million. Four months blaze by, and the high growth startup continues adding new users as fast as it can add capacity. This level of traction creates a buzz in the venture capital community, with an early-stage VC firm signing up for a $3 million round. The startup founders gradually gave up some percentage of their ownership over the several investment rounds. Even so, the ever-increasing valuation of the startup means that the founders each own a smaller percentage of the company pie, but the overall pie has grown much bigger. With luck and hard work, the startup will go on to be acquired by a larger company, with all the shareholders receiving a large return on their investment.

Funding Payback. All of the funding rounds in this scenario are exchanged for a portion of equity (shares) in the startup. The investors own a percentage of the startup and hope the startup is acquired (also called an exit or liquidity event) by a larger company for a large sum of money. Investors receive payback when the proceeds from the acquisition are divided up among the shareholders of the startup—the founders, employees, friends and family investors, angel investors, and VCs.

Example Milestones Supported by Convertible Debt

Consider a convertible note that is structured with a 12-month term. Two things must happen within the next 12 months:

1. **Hit Milestones.** Your startup must reach significant milestones, like paying customers, to increase your chances of convincing next round investors to invest. The convertible debt funding fuels the achievement of these milestones.

2. **Raise Equity Funding.** You must also be in fundraising mode, meaning that you are actively pitching to investors to raise an equity round. Raising capital takes time, so plan on engaging with investors early, keeping them informed of your progress and funding needs.

Following are examples of significant milestones that could support the above two startup goals:

First Paying Customer Milestone. In many cases, investors such as angels or VCs want to see a startup with paying customers, which means you need an early version of your product or service to sell. Using a milestone of your first paying customer is a good way to derive how much to raise in a convertible debt round.

Work backwards from the paying customer milestone and outline the tasks that must be completed to get there—early product version completed, tested with friendly customers, revised and tweaked, and so. Next, estimate the budget needed to complete the tasks and hit the first paying customer milestone. That budget plus a buffer of 50% sets a good goal for the convertible note raise amount.

Enough to Fund One or Two Pivots. Many startups build quick versions of their products and measure how much their potential customers like the product. These Minimal Viable Products (MVP) have limited features and are designed to test whether they really solve a meaningful customer product. If the product benefit does not really resonate with potential customers, the startup often pivots to a new version of the product with features that customers love, or they even discover entirely new products or entirely new customer segments not originally planned.

These quick MVP cycles take time and money, but patient and wise investors bet on good teams that can engage with customer and build innovative products. And, convertible debt is an appropriate funding structure to support the MVP process.

While the costs of MVP/product or market pivot can be difficult to estimate, calculating a rough monthly burn rate of cash gives good basis for the funding needed. Here's an example:

Monthly Burn Rate:	**$15,000**
MVP Cycle Time:	**3 Months**
Total Budget:	**$45,000**
Two Months Buffer:	**$30,000**
Total Raise Amount:	**$75,000**

Enough to Build a Prototype. Many technology focused entrepreneurs use convertible debt to help them complete the proof of concept of new technology. Founders with a proven track record of bringing new technology to market can convince investors to take a big risk to help fund the development of an early prototype and prove out the technology. With a working prototype in hand, it's easier to convince larger scale equity investors like angels or VCs to fund the next stage of the startup. These experienced investors tend to hesitate if there is not something to see that proves a technology or product is more than just an idea—a working prototype, MVP software code, and other product realizations help achieve this goal. Planning your convertible debt funding raise amount around a prototype build fits well with investor goals and expectations.

Develop a detailed plan and budget for the prototype build and testing, and be sure to include your estimates for how much time and money will be needed to move beyond the prototype stage to a customer-ready version of the product. Convertible debt investors will want to know how much funding you'll need to raise in the next round.

One Round of Debt is Enough

Ideally, your funding plan includes only one round of convertible debt. Raising more than one round of convertible debt has many downsides, with the primary red flag being that you are not making enough progress and not hitting key milestones to attract equity investor like angels. Progress toward paying customers is the fuel that causes investors to get excited about the startup's potential and ultimately invest their cash. The primary use of convertible debt is to build enough value in your startup to attract equity investors that can inject larger amounts of cash.

2

Key Moving Parts of a Convertible Note

In this section we review the key parts of a simple convertible note. Keep these elements in mind as you plan your convertible debt funding round.

The Note Amount

This section of the convertible note simply states the total amount of the loan, $50,000 for example. Also called the face value of the note.

Interest Rate

Like a traditional loan, convertible notes carry an interest rate, expressed in an annual amount, and compounded annually as well. Rates of 7% to 10% are common for convertible notes. Also, the interest accrues (accumulates), but the startup does not have to make monthly payments. When the note converts, the accrued interest is added to the principal for the conversion calculation.

Interest rates are typically not heavily negotiated by investors. While the accrued interest on the note does result in additional shares when the debt converts to equity, the amount is relatively small compared to the discount rate (detailed below).

On the other hand, the discount rate can be hotly negotiated, as it has the most leverage in determining the number of shares the convertible note holder (the investor) gets when the note converts.

Maturity Date

The term or duration of the loan is stated in the form of a maturity date. Most convertible notes deals are configured with a 12- or 18-month maturity. Longer maturity dates such as 24 or 30 months are possible, but many investors feel that startups need to move faster than that, pushing for shorter durations.

Remember, the idea is that if things are going well for the startup will be successful in raising the next round of funding, and the note will convert to stock before the maturity date is reached.

What happens of the maturity date is reached and the startup has not closed an equity funding deal? See the later section called "Dealing with Convertible Debt Timing Issues" to review the options.

Conversion Triggers

This section of the convertible note spells out WHEN the note will convert to equity. The key conversion trigger for most convertible notes is the closing of the next round of funding. Other conversion triggers may include the sale of the startup or an IPO, but both of these events are rare for a startup at the early fundraising stage.

Here are examples of typical conversion trigger language found in a convertible note:

On Threshold Financing

The Note will be required to be converted into stock of the Company upon the occurrence of a "Threshold Financing." A "Threshold Financing" will be a sale of stock by the Company (other than to employees, officers, directors, or advisors) aggregating $1,000,000 or more. The conversion will be into stock of the same class and series as issued in the Threshold Financing. The total number of shares into which Note may be converted will be determined by dividing the balance of the Note (principal plus accrued and unpaid interest) by the conversion price which shall be equal to the per share price of the stock issued in the Threshold Financing.

On IPO

The Note will be required to be converted into stock of the Company upon the occurrence of an underwritten initial public offering ("IPO") in which the public offering price is at least $5.00 per share of common stock (or its equivalent) and the gross proceeds to the Company are at least $5,000,000. The total number of shares into which the Note may be converted will be determined by dividing the balance of the Note (principal plus accrued and unpaid interest) by the conversion price which shall be equal to the per share price of the stock issued in the Threshold Financing.

Elective Conversion

The holders of Note may elect to convert the Note into shares of the Company's Series A Preferred Stock or into shares of the Company's common stock at any time such shares may exist if not automatically converted by the "Threshold Financing" paragraph above. The conversion price upon an elective conversion will be at the same rate as the Series A Preferred when created or the then fair market value of the common stock, as applicable.

Conversion Securities

The conversion securities section answers the question of what kind of shares the convertible note holder gets when the convertible note loan converts. It is typical for the note to convert into the same type of shares issued in the next round of financing. Experienced equity investors like angel groups typically define the share type and associated preferences they are willing to accept. The convertible note investor enjoys the benefit of piggybacking with the equity round negotiations.

Here are the typical options for conversion securities:

Common Shares. The basic ownership unit in a startup. (For LLCs the equivalent is usually called a membership unit, but the purpose is the same—defining the basic ownership unit of the corporate entity.)

A convertible note that converts to common shares gives startup founders several advantages:

- More governance and control—voting rights, board seats, and so on

- Reduced exit dilution for founders

- Clean Cap table for future rounds

Preferred Shares. With preferred shares, investors negotiate additional rights tied to their stock shares. The class of shares is assigned a name, such as Series A Preferred. Preferred shares carry certain preferential rights that benefit the investor. Here are a few of the possible preferences tied to a preferred share definition:

- **Participation Preference.** In the event of an exit, preferred holders "participate" with the common shareholders to split up the proceeds of the acquisition, after any liquidation preferences have been fulfilled.

- **Liquidation Preference.** If there is an exit, the investor gets a disbursement of money equal to the invested amount, or a multiple of the original investment, referred to as a 1X (one times), 2X (two times), and so on, liquidation preference. This right is often combined with the participation preference. Most investors do not want to gouge founders, so this point is negotiable.

- **Anti-Dilution Preference.** Versions of this preference protect the investor against a down round, where the current investment round is being executed at a lower valuation than the previous investment round. You and your investors always want your startup valuation to increase. When the pie is getting smaller, investors seek to maintain their current percentage ownership using anti-dilution preferences.

Preferred Share Founder Impact. Preferred shares impact founders in some not so subtle ways:

- Founders give up small degrees of governance and control, such as voting rights and other approvals are needed by the preferred share holders.

- Founders can face substantial exit dilution depending on the big leverage rights like liquidation and participation preferences.

For more details on all of the possible preferred share rights, look for the *Founder's Pocket Guide: Term Sheets and Preferred Shares* at www.1x1media.com

Discount Rate

The discount rate section of the convertible note answers the question of how good the deal is for the convertible note holder. Investors take a high risk of loaning a startup seed stage money and like to be compensated for putting their cash in jeopardy. The discount rate assigned in the convertible note gives the investor a bonus by discounting the share price in the conversion process when the next funding round is closed, ultimately resulting in the note holder getting more shares for his or her money.

Here's an example of how the conversion discount works:

1. ***Start with the key parameters of the deal.*** In this example, convertible note investors have injected $50,000 into the startup with a 20% discount. Several months later the founders negotiate a Series A equity deal resulting in a $1.00 per share price. Here are the key components needed to calculate the conversion share price:

Convertible Note Amount: $50,000

Conversion Discount: 20%

Series A Share Price: $1.00

2. *Calculate the conversion share price.* Simply multiply the conversion discount percentage by the price per share established in the Series A equity round, then subtract the resulting share price discount from the Series A share price.

Conversion Discount Percentage		Series A Share Price		Share Price Discount
20%	×	$1.00	=	$0.20

Series A Share Price		Share Price Discount		Conversion Share Price
$1.00	-	$0.20	=	$0.80

3. *Calculate the number of shares earned when the note converts.* First, add the accrued interest to the total convertible note amount, and then divide by the conversion share price calculated in step 1.

$$\frac{\text{Note Amount} + \text{Accrued Interest}}{\text{Conversion Share Price}} = \text{Number of Shares Note Holder Receives}$$

$$\frac{\$50,000}{\$0.80} = 62,500 \text{ shares}$$

Valuation Cap

Convertible note investors take high risks by funding in early stage startups. Their money, experience, and connections add great value to the startup and make the difference between success and failure. One of the risks of using convertible debt as an investment structure to the investor is the potential for the startup to negotiate a high valuation in the Series A investment round. A high valuation in the next round means that convertible note holder gets a smaller percentage ownership in the startup. The higher the valuation, the lower percentage equity the note holder gets. This chart on the next page shows the impact of a high valuation on the convertible note holder's equity—as the valuation goes up, the note holder's relative ownership percentage goes down.

As the Series A valuation grows,

Pre-Money Valuation	$ 2,000,000	$ 3,000,000	$ 4,000,000
Series A Investment Amount	$ 1,000,000	$ 1,000,000	$ 1,000,000
Post-Money Valuation	$ 3,000,000	$ 4,000,000	$ 5,000,000
Series A Shares	1,000,000	1,000,000	1,000,000
Founders Shares	2,000,000	3,000,000	4,000,000
Note Holder Shares	250,000	250,000	250,000
Total Shares Outstanding	3,250,000	4,250,000	5,250,000
Note Holder's Equity	8%	6%	5%

the convertible note holder's equity declines.

50

A valuation cap defined in the convertible note helps limit this problem for the note holder. When the conversion occurs, the conversion calculation uses the lower valuation cap defined in the convertible note to calculate a conversion discount percentage, which results in the note holder converting the convertible debt into more shares of the Series A stock, thus resulting in less dilution of there investment stake.

Linking Conversion Discount and Valuation Cap

If the convertible debt deal includes a valuation cap, you need to define how the debt conversion is calculated—either using the valuation cap or using the discount rate.

To give the convertible note investor the best deal, most convertible note clauses state that the conversion share price is calculated using the method that results in the lowest share price, giving the investor the best possible deal, and larger number of shares earned in the equity funding round.

3

Dealing with Convertible Debt Timing Issues

There are a few problematic outcomes for both startup founders and investors due to the time limited nature of the convertible note structure. The clock is ticking toward the maturity date of the convertible note, and conversely, the clock can be accelerated by early acquisition interest in the startup. These timing issues bring up two questions that should be answered at beginning of your convertible note discussions with investors:

1. Out of Time. What happens if the maturity date is reached and the startup has not closed it's next funding round, thus triggering the conversion of the note debt into equity?

2. Early Acquisition. What happens if the startup is very successful, very early, and gets acquired by a large company prior to the convertible note conversion—what happens to the convertible note holder's debt?

The next sections detail how these issues are typically managed.

Issue 1: Maturity Date Reached, No Equity Round

What happens if the convertible note's maturity date arrives before the founders close an equity financing round?

In this scenario, the startup has not been successful in raising an equity round to trigger the conversion of the convertible debt. In the wording of a typical convertible note, the total convertible debt amount is due to be repaid, plus interest. This is not what either the investor not the founders really wants to occur. Here are the options for resolving the situation.

Solution 1. The Startup Pays the Note Back with Interest. In most cases, a startup in this situation will be unable to pay back the convertible note debt. The company likely has little cash available. And if any cash is available, spending it to repay the note holders likely means the end of the startup— no cash, no startup.

Repayment is not the best option for investors, either. They put their money to work hoping to generate a larger return when the startup becomes successful, so a payback results in a smaller than hoped for return. If repayment is possible and accepted, most founders and investors chalk the situation up to lessons learned.

Solution 2. Extend the Maturity Date. Negotiating a new maturity date for the convertible debt loan is the most practical solution to a timed-out convertible note. It's a situation neither the investor nor the founders want to be in, but many times it's in the investor's best interest to give the founders more time to reach milestones and convince new investors to fund an equity round.

The startup most likely will be in one of three positions that would impact the decision about whether or not to extend the maturity date:

A. **Close to a deal.** Close to closing an equity deal, just need more time to get the deal done. In this case, it's clear that convertible note holders will be motivated to extend the maturity date.

B. **Deal possible, but not in sight.** In this middle ground, an equity deal is possible, pitches are underway, but new investors would like to see more milestone/validations before pulling the trigger. Convertible note holders usually allow more time to see if a deal can be closed.

C. **No equity deal in sight.** In this unhappy situation, the startup is struggling to hit key milestones such as completing an early version of their product, convincing customers to sign up, and ultimately validating that the market cares about their product. If time is up on the convertible note and few key validations are logged, convertible note holders may seek to fall back to seeking repayment of the note and interest.

Solution 3. Automatic Conversion Into Equity on Maturity. With this solution, the convertible note specifies a that the convertible debt converts into some form of equity in the startup, regardless of the status of the next equity round. There are two basic share types that convertible debt can convert into—common shares or preferred shares. Founders benefit most if the convertible note debt converts to common shares, avoiding giving the note holders preferred rights and potentially more governance and control in the startup. Converting to common shares upon the maturity of the note is a little unfair to the investor. They were banking on the founders raising a successful next round of equity funding and receiving the same preferred shares as the Series A investors.

In this instance, the convertible note has reached the maturity date and the note requires the loan amount to convert to equity in the startup. Normally, all of the equity deal parameters (valuation, security type) are dictated by the next round financing, but in this case, there is no next round. So the valuation of the startup needs to be negotiated between the founders and the convertible note holders, as well as the types of shares convertible note holders will receive.

Issue 2: Early Acquisition of the Startup

What happens if the startup is acquired before an equity financing round is completed? Acquisition is usually broadly defines include a merger, change of control, or sale of the assets of the startup.

Early acquisition is usually driven by two causes:

Red Hot Startup. The startup is red hot, adding users or customers at a rapid pace and getting attention for its early success. In this instance, an early acquisition probably means a very attractive acquisition offer has been made, enticing founders and other stakeholders (like the convertible note holders) to consider cashing out early. Note holders need to protect themselves to the upside, negotiating provisions that allow them to share in the early success of the startup.

Floundering Startup. In the case of a startup that has difficulty reach the next plateau of success, such as consistently adding new customers, founders sometimes seek to find a way out. Merging or selling off the startup with another more successful and complementary company can be the right conclusion for the startup.

No matter what the cause of an early acquisition or merger, convertible note holders need to protect themselves against the downside circumstances by including provisions that spell out what happens if the startup is acquired before conversion.

The note holders have three options to protect themselves in the case of an early acquisition of the startup:

1. **Right to get paid back**

2. **Conversion right**

3. **Change of control provision**

Let's have a look at each of these solutions:

Solution 1. Right to Get Paid Back the Convertible Debt Plus Interest. In this solution, the Note includes provisions to accelerate the maturity date of the note to coincide with the closing of the startup's acquisition, and the total amount of the loan, plus interest, is due. This outcome is not as favorable to the convertible debt investors, who want a high return on their investment, not just the interest earned on the convertible debt. Most experienced investors will not agree to this option. They took the high risk of putting money in the startup at its early stages, and will push for deal options that reward them for taking the risk and helping grow the startup.

Solution 2. Conversion Right. If the startup is getting acquired by another company, a purchase price and valuation will be established, and consequently a price per share for the startup's stock. The conversion right clause of the convertible note can give the note holder (the investor) the option to convert his/her debt investment into the priced stock shares established during the early acquisition.

Conversion may or may not be a good option, depending on the acquisition deal. If the startup is acquired for a large premium, the conversion might be lucrative for the convertible note holder. If the startup is acquired for a modest or even small amount, the conversion might be a bad deal for the convertible note holder depending on the amount of the convertible note. In many cases, the conversion right is an "either/or" option, giving the note holder the option to choose the better deal between conversion, pay back, or change of control premium, as explained next.

Solution 3. Change of Control Provision. A change of control provision offers the convertible note holder the option to get the investment paid back if the startup gets acquired before the note converts to equity.

In many instances, the change of control provision requires the convertible note investment to be repaid at a multiple of the original convertible note amount in the event of change of control of the startup. For example, a provision might require a change of control payment of 1X or 2X of the principal and accrued interest if the startup us acquired before the note converts.

Change of control is defined as the acquisition of the company by another entity such as a merger or consolidation, or the sale of the material assets of the startup, such as patents and other IP.

A change of control provision can be problematic for founders if the startup is being sold for a low amount. Consider a $200,000 convertible note with a 2X change of control premium triggered by a startup being sold at fire sale pricing of $250,000. The 2X premium owed the convertible note holders is more than the proceeds from the sale.

Of course these difficulties can be accounted for with endless what-if legal clauses, but that's usually not the best use of your legal spending.

Be aware of what a change of control premium is and if the convertible note investor insists on one, work with your lawyer to arrive at a solution the helps move the deal forward without sweating the what-if scenarios. Sorry to say, but's it's exceedingly rare for a startup to get acquired so early in its existence, so this is one for founders to give in on if the investor is a good fit otherwise.

4

Using Convertible Debt for Your Startup

This section reviews several practical aspects of using the convertible debt structure to raise capital for your new venture, including step by step guidelines, convertible debt term sheet provisions, and cautions and pitfalls.

Raising Funds with Convertible Debt, Step by Step

This section reviews the high level steps for raising a convertible debt funding round.

1. *Document your funding plan.* Start by outlining the key milestones, supporting tasks, estimated timing, resources needed, and ultimately the budget/cost of each phase of your plan. A good funding plan includes the following items:

   Key milestones to be achieved. Big achievements that clearly show the startup is implementing its big ideas. Example milestones include: Completing an MVP and getting customer feedback, signing up your first 100 (or 1,000) customers, signing an early adopter agreement with a major account, getting regulatory approval for your new device, and so on.

Tasks. Working backwards from the key milestones, list the high level tasks that need to be accomplished to achieve the milestones.

Timing. Estimate the amount of time needed to carry out the tasks, and ultimately the key milestones. Be sure to keep an eye on the overall timeline and make sure it fits with the maturity date of your convertible note financing plan—a 24 month timeline overlaid with a 18 month convertible note doesn't match.

Resources. More detailed funding plans include a section that outlines the types of resources needed to accomplish task and hit milestones, including founders' input/work, contractors, outsourced coding/development partners, interns, and so on. Resource types dictate the budget/cost tied to each portion of the plan.

Budget and Raise Amount. Once you've made good guesses about milestones, tasks, timing, and resources, estimate the budget needed to fund each phase of the plan.

Buffers. Be sure to build in extra time and extra money for each phase or step of the plan. As anybody knows, in startups and in life, plans never quite materialize as you expect. A minimum buffer might include 25% more time and money, and a really safe buffer could approach 50 to 75% more time and money.

2. *Establish the details of the convertible note.* With your funding plan in hand, next outline the key elements of the convertible debt funding you plan to raise. Details include: Total raise amount, interest rate, discount rate, maturity date, and types of shares.

Note Maturity

Remember you have to get two big things done using the convertible debt funding—hit milestones in your startup, such as building a MVP of your product, and woo the next round of equity investors to help fund the growth of the company. Be sure to build in enough time to enable you to accomplish your startup milestones, and add in a 3- to 6-month buffer as a safety margin. You don't want to risk running out of time and having to renegotiate the terms of the convertible note.

3. ***Create a basic cap table.*** Even though you are not giving up equity in your startup via the convertible note (now), it's a good idea to include the convertible note details in a simple cap table. A cap table is typically an Excel spreadsheet that tracks the equity ownership of the startup—who owns how many shares, and how much cash has been invested, calculating the resulting ownership percentages of the founders and outside investors.

4. ***Be prepared to discuss the conversion discount and valuation cap.*** A valuation cap provision in the convertible note helps limit the amount of dilution the convertible note holders incur. And the conversion discount directly influences how many more shares the convertible note holder gets for the convertible note invested amount. Plan to review the basics of these factors before entering detailed discussions with investors.

5. *Prepare the basic legal documents with your lawyer.* While some of the finer points of the convertible note documents are likely to get negotiated during your investor discussions, you'll want to prepare a basic set of legal documents for the convertible debt deal. Lean on your experienced startup lawyer to help prepare these documents.

6. *Create a hit list of potential investors.* Most cities of even modest size have numerous events and support resources designed to help startup founders get connected and raise money. Examples include angel groups and networks, startup networking events, founder networking forums, startup pitch competitions, business incubators, and startup accelerators. Use these resources to locate and get introduced to potential investors. Once you've picked your targets, do some basic research on the potential investors—are they accredited, have they invested in startups before, can they add value to your startup effort beyond money, and so on?

Accredited Investors

It is best to limit convertible note and equity investment deals to accredited investors only. If you have unaccredited investors on your hit list, attempt to structure their investments as loans, gifts, or even presales of your product (à la crowdfunding.)

The SEC defines an accredited investor (under Rule 501 of Reg D: http://www.sec.gov/answers/regd.htm) as:

1. a natural person who has individual net worth, or joint net worth with the person's spouse, that exceeds $1 million, excluding the value of the primary residence of such person, or

2. a natural person with income exceeding $200,000 in each of the two most recent years or joint income with a spouse exceeding $300,000 for those years and a reasonable expectation of the same income level in the current year

The SEC accredited investor criteria are designed to help protect both investors and companies seeking investors. Investors that meet the wealth hurdles have the money to lose (in theory), and entrepreneurs raising money for their startup have some assurance that the investors have money to put at risk.

7. *Make investor pitches.* Get warm referrals if possible. Be prepared with your pitch deck and other supporting tools such as financial model, business plan, customer and sales funnel, key metrics. Many founders use their funding road map to show potential investors how the convertible note funding will enable them to hit significant milestones and ultimately raise their next round of equity funding.

8. *Move through due diligence.* With investors convinced to inject their cash into your plan, the next step is likely some light due diligence. Investors will ask more detailed questions, review your projections

and implementation plans, meet your co-founders and early staff, and generally get more comfortable with your startup.

Due diligence for a convertible note deal can often be quick. Experienced investors know that there is not much to look at in early-stage startups. At the same time, do your own due diligence on the investor—do they have a good reputation in the community, are your personalities compatible, are they accredited, can they help open doors to bigger opportunities, and so on.

9. ***Negotiate the details and set a closing date(s).*** Negotiate the details of the convertible note. As related earlier, the maturity date and discount rate are likely to be the main factors discussed. Keep you eye on the right goal—getting funded for this phase and then jump back into the fun of building the startup. Negotiating over a few percentage points is probably not the best use of your time.

Consistent Deal Terms

It may take several investors to complete your total convertible note raise amount. Keeping the deal terms consistent across all investors makes it easier to track and manage, as well as simplify your overall capitalization structure, leading to smoother fundraising in the next equity round.

10. Keep raising money. If you haven't met your convertible debt funding goal, say you've raised $200,000 of a goal of $500,000, then keep making pitches. Consider adding deal sweeteners such as deeper discount rates for the investors that come in early. The longer they wait, the lower the discount rate on the convertible note.

11. Keep investors updated. Once you've reached your fundraising goal and have returned to building the startup, keep investors updated on your progress. Plan on sending written updated at least once per quarter. Items to include in investor updates include:

- **Headlines.** Lead off with short status updates about major initiatives, milestones missed or hit, major customers or partnership opportunities.

- **Technology/Product Development.** Share the status of product development, beta tests, IP opportunities, setbacks or leaps ahead.

- **Financial Condition.** Cover the key financial metrics, including actual versus forecasted revenues, cash on hand, current burn rate, monthly and year-to-date revenues compared to your forecast. Also note any major changes to expenses and progress toward break-even.

- **Funding/Capital Raising.** If additional fundraising rounds are underway, provide the status of fund raising goals and activities and whether there are issues, concerns, or major changes.

- **Sales and Marketing.** Detail key customers landed, important opportunities, major marketing initiatives, and other activities that influence the sales success of the company.

What Happens When a Convertible Note Converts?

Experienced founders take the time to walk potential investors through the details of how a convertible note funding structure plays out, including the discount rate, trigger event, and ultimately the conversion of the debt investment into equity ownership in the startup.

The following scenario illustrates a detailed convertible note funding round as well as the next equity funding round and convertible note conversion.

The Convertible Note Funding Round

Let's walk through a convertible note with the following terms:

- **Note Amount: $50,000.** Startup raises $50,000 in the form of a convertible note from an accredited investor.

- **Interest rate: 10%.** The parties agree to a 10% interest rate on the convertible note. The interest will accrue annually and no monthly payments will be paid.

- **Discount Rate: 20%.** The parties agree to a 20% discount. The convertible note investor will receive a 20% discount on the share price established at the next equity funding round.

- **Trigger Event: Next Equity Round.** The note conversion will trigger at the next round of equity investment, when a valuation will be established for the startup.

- **Type of Securities: Same as Next Round Investors.** The convertible note will convert into the same class of shares given to the next round investors. If the angel investors negotiate preferred shares with favorable rights and preferences, then convertible note holder will also get preferred shares.

- **Valuation: Not Established.** No valuation is needed at the convertible note stage. The startup is very early in the development of its product and market, and it's just too early to place a value on the company.

After closing on the convertible note deal with the investor, the startup has $50,000 in the bank and uses it to finish the development of its product and get several early adopter customers using it and raving about it.

The First Equity Funding Round

Next, with several key milestones achieved using the convertible note funding, the founders start raising their first angel round, convincing an organized angel group to invest. The founders and angels agree to the following investment parameters:

- **Angel Round:** $250,000 to be invested

- **Pre-Money Valuation:** $500,000

- **Post-Money Valuation:** $750,000 ($500,000 pre-money + $250,000 invested = $750,000)

- **Angel Ownership Percentage:** 33% ($250,000 invested / $750,000 post-money = 33%)

- **Security Type:** Preferred shares (specific rights omitted here for brevity)

The Convertible Note Conversion

So what happens to the convertible note holder's $50,000 investment? Here's how the convertible note converts:

- **Angel Share Price: $1.00.** The share price results from the share price math at the end of the angel round closing. (The $1 price represents a simplified example; in reality, it's unlikely the share price would be an even $1.)

- **Angel Shares: 250,000.** Angels get 250,000 shares for their $250,000 invested.

- **Share Price with Convertible Note Discount: $0.80.** The convertible note specifies a 20% discount, so the convertible note investor shares can be purchased for $0.80 each ($1.00 share - $0.20 discount = $0.80), as compared to the $1.00 per share paid by the angel investors.

- **Total Shares to the convertible note Investor: 62,500.** Therefore the convertible note investor's $50,000 investment buys 62,500 shares ($50,000 / $.80 share price = 62,500) The 20% discount earned the investor an extra 12,500 shares.

Calculating the Resulting Equity Ownership

The angels invested $250,000 on a pre-money valuation of $500,000, resulting in a 33% ownership stake ($250,000/$750,000 post = 33% ownership).

The convertible note investor owns 62,500 shares/750,000 total outstanding shares = 8.3%.

The founders own the remaining 58.7% of the company.

If the startup goes on to bigger things and ultimately gets acquired, then the convertible note investor's risky investment could pay off, especially since he or she owns the same preferred shares the angels negotiated.

Convertible Note Term Sheet Deal Points

A term sheet documents the high level points of the convertible debt deal and is usually only one or two pages long. Deal points include the loan amount, the interest rate, the maturity date, and the discount rate. Additional rights of the investors and requirements of the startup are also included in the term sheet, such as who pays the legal fees of the deal, and any insurance requirements for key founders.

Using a term sheet provides both founders and investors a place to document the details of the investment deal, and document proposals and counter proposals. Working with a short term sheet document speeds up the process and eliminates the need to exchange and revise the more lengthy Note Purchase Agreement and the Convertible Note document itself. If you can't come to an agreement on the points in the term sheet, there is no need to move on the other more complex documents. While the terms sheets are signed to signal agreement between the two parties, they are typically not legally binding. In other words, he deal is not complete until the investor's check clears.

Not Done Yet—Term Sheet Signing

Just because you have a signed term sheet doesn't mean the deal is done. The term sheet on any investment deal is an "agreement in principle," meaning it is not legally binding. Several additional legal contracts need to be executed before both parties are legally bound to the terms of the deal—the promissory note that details the convertible debt obligation, a note purchase agreement, and sometimes a security agreement that details any collateral obligations of the deal. Founder's can truly relax (and celebrate) when the check is deposited in your bank account.

Examining Example Term Sheet Provisions

In addition to outlining the basic parameters of the convertible note deal, several other conditions can make the list:

Prepayment. Prepaying the convertible note loan would be counter to the motivations of the investor. They want the note to convert to equity and see a large return on their investment. Forbidding prepayment is not unexpected.

Example Wording:

> "The Convertible Note may not be prepaid without the consent of the note holder."

Security Interest. This provision offers the investor a small degree of security by naming the assets of the startup as collateral for the convertible note loan.

Remember that a convertible note is considered a debt instrument in the eyes of the law, and debt holders often require collateral as a means to secure their investment in case the debt can't be repaid.

In the case of a convertible note, the investor really doesn't want the note to be paid back or take possession of equipment, IP, or other assets of the startup, but rather prefers it to convert to equity.

Example Wording:

"The Notes shall be secured by a first lien on all tangible and intangible assets of the company."

Board of Directors Observer Rights. Unlike certain rights attached to preferred share equity owners, convertible note holders do not have any control or governance in the startup. To offset this lack of control, convertible note term sheets will often include a clause allowing an observer at the startup's board of directors meetings. The convertible note board observer doesn't have any say or vote at the meeting, but at least they can have a front row seat to key decisions being made at the meetings.

Example Wording:

"The note holder will have the right to appoint one observer to attend each board meeting of the startup."

Legal Fees. This section of the term sheet states which party pays the legal fees associated with the investment deal. It's common or the startup to pay the legal fees, but they can use some of the proceeds of the investment to do so.

Example wording:

"The Company will bear all legal and other expenses with respect to the negotiation and closing of the Convertible Note, including reasonable fees and expenses of counsel to the Investors and related due diligence expenses incurred by the Investors.

The amount of proceeds from the Convertible Note that may be used by the Company to pay for transaction fees and expenses shall be capped at 5% of the face amount of the Convertible Note, and all other transaction fees and expenses shall be paid by the principals of the Company. All transaction documents relating to the issuance of the Convertible Note shall be prepared by counsel for the Investors."

Key Man Insurance. Many early-stage startups are brought to life by the vision and passion of a single founder. Over time, this founder attracts co-founders and other key employees to help transform the vision and idea into something tangible that customers/users love. In many cases, the loss of the visionary founder kills the startup entirely. Investors mitigate this risk by requiring the startup to secure a Key Man life insurance policy. If the key man dies, the investor has some chance of recouping a portion of his investment via the insurance policy.

Example wording:

"The Company will have obtained "key man" life insurance on the lives of *Your Name Here* in an amount not less than $1,000,000, naming the Company as beneficiary."

Founder Employment Agreements. Often part of the "deferred housekeeping" that founders put off until they are forced to, this clause requires founders to establish and sign legally binding employment and noncompete agreements with the startup. An experienced startup legal firm will have boilerplate agreements that cover founder employment agreements, non compete agreements, and invention assignment agreements.

Example Wording:

"As a condition to this Convertible Note, the Company must have entered into a binding Employment Agreement, with noncompete provisions."

Convertible Debt Cautions and Pitfalls

Raising startup funds in the form of convertible debt forms a solid middle ground of effort, expense, and upside for all parties involved, and therefore a good option for startup founders to pursue. Keep the following additional factors in mind of you are planning a convertible debt deal:

- **Not Too Small.** Raising a small amount of funding with a convertible note, such as issuing a $5,000 convertible note to Uncle Larry, is probably not worth the time and expense. In contrast, raising a round using a convertible note in the range of $20,000 to $100,000 balances the effort and expense with a solid amount of startup capital raised.

- **Not Too Many.** Just as an early-stage startup shouldn't take on too many friends and family funders at the very early stages of your new venture, similarly avoid taking on lots of convertible note holders. You don't want to have to track down and get approvals and signatures from several convertible note holders in order to close a bigger funding deal with angel investors. Wading through murky waters like this can quickly kill the next level deal. A general rule of thumb is to limit convertible note holders to fewer than three to five. More than that starts to get difficult to manage.

- **Non-Voting Shares.** If the convertible note holder is unaccredited, consider having the note convert to non-voting common shares. Experienced investors that bring larger funding rounds to startup (think $250,000 or more) usually require preferred shares be created to represent their ownership interest in the company. The preferred shares carry certain rights that help protect the investor, provide more control in certain situations like shareholder voting, and ultimately dictate how the money gets divided in the event of a successful exit. Limiting unaccredited convertible note holders to non-voting common shares helps keep the cap table clean for the next round of accredited equity investors.

Thank You

This concludes the *Founder's Pocket Guide: Convertible Debt.* We hope you find our content and supporting tools useful for your startup journey.

We are always looking for feedback on our startup tools. If you have comments, feedback, or corrections, please send us a note.

info@1x1media.com

http://www.1x1media.com

#

Made in the USA
Monee, IL
06 June 2023

35348664R00046